THESE
THREE
THINGS

A DAILY JOURNAL

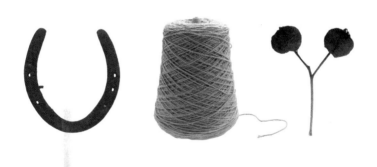

LISA ANDERSON SHAFFER

RUNNING PRESS
PHILADELPHIA

Molly
love

Running Press
Hachette Book Group
1290 Avenue of the Americas, New York, NY 10104
www.runningpress.com
@Running_Press

Printed in China

Published by Running Press, an imprint of Perseus Books, LLC, a subsidiary of Hachette Book Group, Inc. The Running Press name and logo is a trademark of the Hachette Book Group.

The Hachette Speakers Bureau provides a wide range of authors for speaking events. To find out more, go to www.hachettespeakersbureau.com or call (866) 376-6591.

The publisher is not responsible for websites (or their content) that are not owned by the publisher.

Print book cover and interior design by Susan Van Horn.

Library of Congress Control Number: 2018947860

ISBN: 978-0-7624-6529-3

1010

10 9 8 7 6 5 4 3 2 1

There is never enough time. In the day, in
the week, in the year, and with the ones we love.
If you are waiting for the right time, grab the bull
by the horns and make it the right time.
The right time is the morning you wake up
full of breath and able to live another day.

• • •

WHAT DID YOU LEARN WHEN YOU MADE
TIME FOR WHAT MATTERS MOST?

one _____

_____

_____

_____

_____

_____

_____

_____

_____

two _____

_____

_____

combination of words and images, I maintained the practice for an entire year and have continued even beyond that initial milestone.

Beyond regaining my curiosity, the practice of taking a moment of focus each evening—to fully metabolize what has happened and capture the day's events as invaluable lessons learned—has been an incredible gift. Giving myself an invitation to be curious, to have hope, and to be open to what the day can bring has been not only a wonderful way to get to know myself, but also a way to more deeply connect with loved ones and the world.

This book is a collection of my favorite lessons learned from my daily practice and a way for you to begin your own. Some lessons were fun, many were difficult, but all of them have encouraged and strengthened my sense of curiosity. Though this journal won't take you through a full year, it will jump start your creative energy. Some of the pages begin with my own observations about the world, and questions to help you reflect on the topics that have resonated with me. Other pages simply offer space for you to record your own musings, taking inspiration from your day and the world around you. I hope that this book acts as an inspiring guide for your own daily practice of self-discovery and that you too will revel in the wonder and the curiosity of all that there is to be learned in this life.

The next day, I entered the studio with a clean slate, leaving all assumptions at the door. Following my intuition, I sat down to write, the least likely of starting points for a person who usually paints herself out of corners. What emerged from that day of writing was the first official post for *These Three Things*—a list of three lessons learned that I knew deep in my bones; sentiments that remained unchanged and unshaken; things that I knew to be true no matter what the world around me was reflecting back. As a visual pairing with my words, I created a photo collage of three separate images, drawn from a collection of photographs I had been taking of natural items found in the area around my mountain home, along with images of heirloom tools and other sentimental keepsakes.

Knowing there had to be others out there feeling weary and worn down, I shared the post on social media. Soon after, friends and friends of friends were responding to my words. With little hesitation, I committed to continue the practice of writing on a daily basis and sharing it publicly with my friends, family, and Zelma Rose followers. Presenting my fine art photography in collections of three things, along with listing three things I learned each day, remained an effortless practice and something that became quite necessary as the next 365 days progressed. Amazed and inspired by the responses from people all over the world, who looked forward to the daily

INTRODUCTION

IT WAS MY FAVORITE KIND OF CALIFORNIA DAY—
a blissful and warm summer morning in July. The
sun was streaming through my studio windows,
but I sat uninspired. For weeks, I had felt my
imagination was out of reach. There were terrible
things going on in the world, both near and far,
and I had grown weary.

I had lost my curiosity. Without curiosity I was
stuck, uninspired, inflexible, and completely vanilla.

For a parent, this is not good. For an artist,
this is a disaster. And as a psychotherapist, there
are few things more frustrating than being unable
to change your own frame of mind. I had helped
many people through their own moments of emotional unrest. Why couldn't I help myself? It turns
out I knew what to do, I just hadn't found the right
way to do it yet.

To start, I decided to seek out what I had
lost. My aim was to reignite my curiosity—to feel
inspired, resolved, and rejuvenated at the day's
end. I was determined to show my daughter that
even during times of seemingly insurmountable
grief and chaos, life can be rich, meaningful, and
rife with good surprises. I was going to remain
curious about life. I committed to stay optimistic
and continue to turn over every stone, even when
life was making me feel like hiding under a rock.

three

one

two

three

DATE:

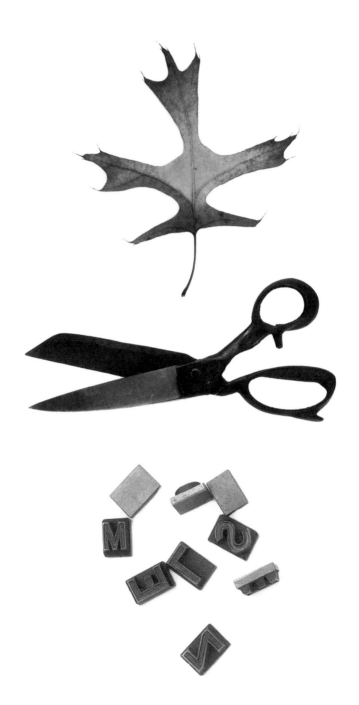

Everything will change.
EVERYTHING.
Your relationships,
your mind, your wisdom,
beauty, friendships, body,
health, job, finances,
home . . . all of it.
Some changes are
for the better,
some are not,
but life is more fun
if you surrender
to this fact.

WHAT DID YOU LEARN ABOUT
ACCEPTING CHANGE IN YOUR LIFE?

one
_____

_____

_____

_____

_____

two
_____

_____

_____

_____

three
_____

_____

_____

_____

DATE: _____

You can ask for what you want in life, but you don't get to decide how and when you get it. If you are waiting for a door to open, keep your eyes on the windows, the chimney, and the gutters. Life presents many possibilities when you are open to embracing unexpected opportunities.

• • •

WHAT DID YOU LEARN WHEN YOU WERE OPEN TO UNEXPECTED POSSIBILITIES?

one
_____

_____

_____

_____

_____

_____

_____

_____

_____

two
_____

_____

_____

three

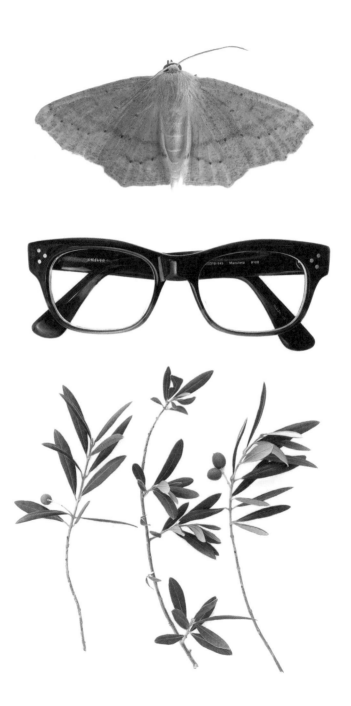

one
_____

_____

_____

_____

_____

two
_____

_____

_____

_____

three
_____

_____

_____

_____

DATE:
_____

The greatest connection you can share with another person is history. Don't underestimate the value of the people in your life who have witnessed all of your metamorphoses. They really know you. All of you. And that is truly incredible.

• • •

one _____

_____

_____

_____

_____

_____

_____

_____

_____

two _____

_____

_____

three

It doesn't have to be pretty. The deepest and most valuable lessons I've learned in this life have been messy as hell, raw to the bone. Once in a while, the lessons come in a glamorous dressing, but most of the time the magic is in the mess.

• • •

WHAT DID YOU LEARN WHILE BEING FACEDOWN IN THE DIRT?

one

_____

_____

_____

_____

_____

_____

_____

_____

two

_____

_____

three

TODAY I LEARNED

one _____

_____

_____

_____

_____

two _____

_____

_____

_____

three _____

_____

_____

_____

DATE: _____

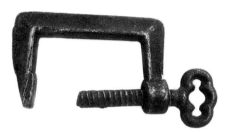

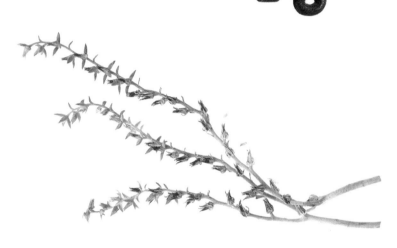

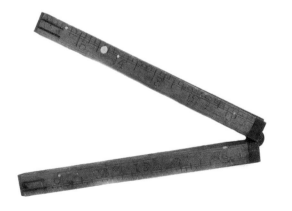

Humans and chimpanzees share 98% of the same DNA. Let that one sink in. This says a lot about small changes, though. That 2% difference is pretty significant. Here's to making seemingly small, teeny-tiny changes that can make a big impact.

• • •

WHAT DID YOU LEARN ABOUT SMALL CHANGES THAT MAKE A DRAMATIC DIFFERENCE?

one _____

_____

_____

_____

_____

_____

_____

_____

two _____

_____

_____

three

Record the
good moments.
Feel them in your heart,
let them sink deep
into your bones.
Let those moments
change you,
for they will pass
way too quickly.

WHAT DID YOU LEARN ABOUT
YOUR OWN MILESTONES?

one
_____

_____

_____

_____

_____

two
_____

_____

_____

_____

_____

three
_____

_____

_____

_____

_____

DATE:
_____

Go ahead and be scared. Often times we get too caught up in the act of being scared. We want to avoid fear, when in reality that's impossible. Everyone is scared of something, and we all still carry on regardless. Just decide to be scared. Chances are everyone else is too.

• • •

WHAT DID YOU LEARN ABOUT YOUR OWN FEARS?

one
_____
_____
_____
_____
_____
_____
_____
_____
_____

two
_____
_____
_____

three

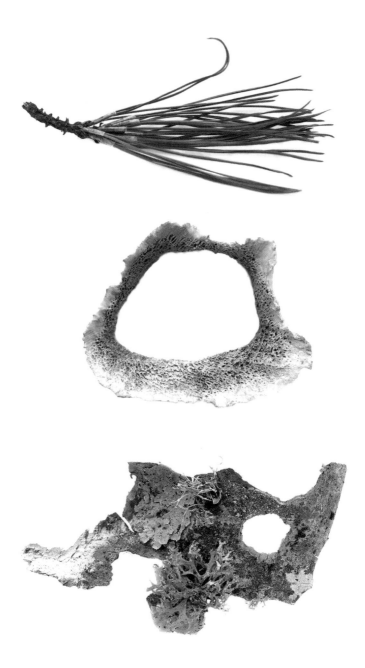

TODAY I LEARNED

one

_____

_____

_____

_____

two

_____

_____

_____

_____

three

_____

_____

_____

_____

DATE: _____

There is an ashram in India where the yogis
take great delight and joy in challenges.
They pray for challenges and see facing obstacles
as an opportunity to further fulfill their dharma.
What an endeavor it would be, to reach
this height of being! In the meantime, it's nice to
think about approaching trials with delight.

• • •

**WHAT DID YOU LEARN ABOUT HOW
YOU FACE CHALLENGES?**

one
_____

_____

_____

_____

_____

_____

_____

_____

two
_____

_____

three

TODAY I LEARNED

one
_____

_____

_____

_____

_____

two
_____

_____

_____

_____

three
_____

_____

_____

_____

DATE: _____

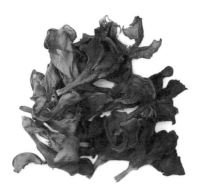

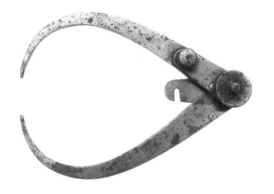

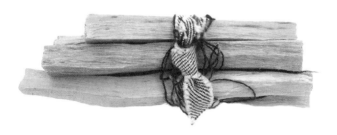

The freedom to celebrate
in another's joy with complete
abandon is its own gift.

WHAT DID YOU LEARN WHEN YOU REJOICED
IN A FRIEND'S HAPPINESS?

one
_____

_____

_____

_____

_____

two
_____

_____

_____

_____

_____

three
_____

_____

_____

_____

_____

DATE:
_____

Save handwritten letters from those you love.
You will never regret seeing their handwriting,
feeling the paper between your fingers, taking in
the depth that the pen created as they pressed
down to write each letter, and being able to touch
the words they have written.

• • •

**WHAT DID YOU LEARN ABOUT THE
THINGS YOU CHERISH?**

one _____

_____

_____

_____

_____

_____

_____

_____

two _____

_____

_____

three

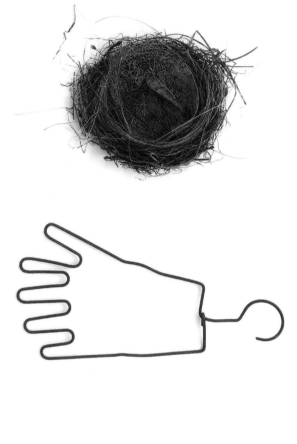
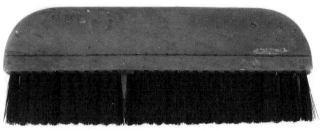

TODAY I LEARNED

one
_____

_____

_____

_____

_____

two
_____

_____

_____

_____

three
_____

_____

_____

_____

_____

DATE:
_____

Do not be deceived by the delivery. Worthwhile lessons come from messengers of all kinds. If we close ourselves off to the message because the messenger or method of delivery is outside our comfort zone, or does not meet our expectations, we miss a whole hell of a lot.

• • •

WHAT DID YOU LEARN ABOUT BEING OPEN TO UNLIKELY MESSENGERS?

one
_____

_____

_____

_____

_____

_____

_____

_____

_____

_____

two
_____

_____

_____

three

Make friends with people who share your trade or work. There is intense joy in discussing the way a particular tool feels in the hand, the quality of a certain supply, and the often unseen details of how you do what you do. It is wonderful to revel in the passion of your process.

• • •

WHAT DID YOU LEARN ABOUT YOUR WORK THAT BRINGS YOU JOY?

one _____

_____

_____

_____

_____

_____

_____

_____

_____

_____

two _____

_____

_____

three

TODAY I LEARNED

one
_____

_____

_____

_____

_____

two
_____

_____

_____

_____

three
_____

_____

_____

_____

DATE: _____

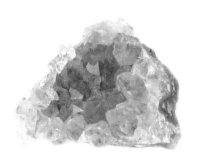

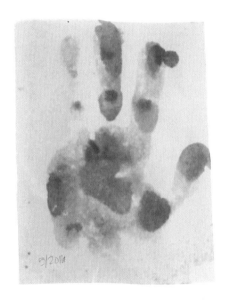

2/2016

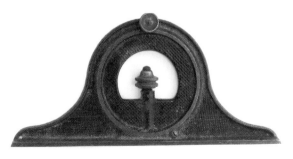

"Me first" is the correct order of things.
I've learned that I'm no good to anyone else
unless I take good care of myself.

• • •

one
_____

_____

_____

_____

_____

_____

_____

_____

_____

two
_____

_____

_____

three

DATE:

It is incredible, the way a tree can bend, sometimes with winds forcing it in many directions at once. We assume we can predict when, and if, the tree will break—during a storm, a gust of wind, a pounding rain. But more often than not, the tree weathers the storm. And one calm day, after the rain, after the gusts of wind, the tree breaks quietly, softly folding over a neighbor's fence. As if to say, "I did it, and that was my destiny."

• • •

WHAT DID YOU LEARN ABOUT YOUR OWN NEED FOR REST IN MOMENTS OF GREAT UPHEAVAL?

one

two

three

DATE:

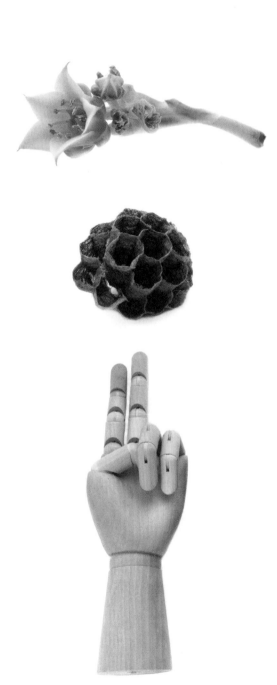

TODAY I LEARNED

one
_____

_____

_____

_____

_____

two
_____

_____

_____

_____

_____

three
_____

_____

_____

_____

_____

DATE: _____

The only true promise is this:
it's all temporary.
Life is incredibly beautiful
precisely because nothing lasts.
So give pause to the good
moments, and know that
the bad moments, the ones
that pit you against
your patience and test your
strength, will soon
become the stories you tell.

WHAT DID YOU LEARN ABOUT THE TEMPORARY NATURE OF YOUR BIG LIFE MOMENTS?

one
_____

_____

_____

_____

two
_____

_____

_____

_____

three
_____

_____

_____

_____

DATE:
_____

Never waste an opportunity, whether it has
been granted to you or fought for. When a door
opens just a few inches, pry it open a few more,
and take others with you.

• • •

one
_____

_____

_____

_____

_____

_____

_____

_____

_____

two
_____

_____

_____

three

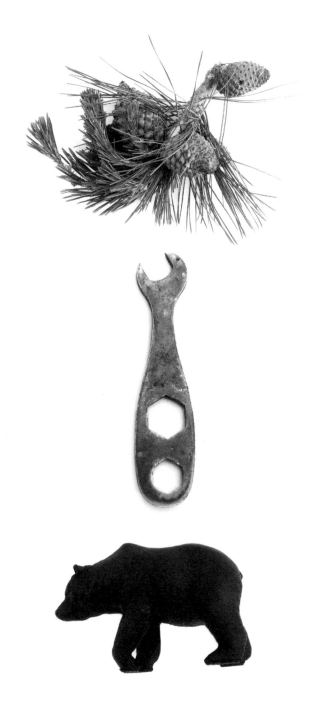

TODAY I LEARNED

one _____

_____

_____

_____

_____

two _____

_____

_____

_____

_____

three _____

_____

_____

_____

_____

DATE: _____

In order for an arrow to take flight, there needs to be an enormous amount of tension on the bow. The greater the tension, the farther the arrow will fly. To move forward, you must first pull back— but do so with aim. During times of chaos and challenge, never lose sight of your aim.

• • •

WHAT DID YOU LEARN ABOUT TAKING A STEP BACKWARD TO MOVE FORWARD?

one
_____
_____
_____
_____
_____
_____
_____
_____
_____

two
_____
_____
_____

three

Be an ally and ask how you can support a friend during a difficult time. Life brings enough drama on a good day. A simple gesture can be the difference between holding on and falling apart.

● ● ●

one
_____

_____

_____

_____

_____

_____

_____

_____

two
_____

_____

_____

_____

three

TODAY I LEARNED

one
_____

_____

_____

_____

_____

two
_____

_____

_____

_____

three
_____

_____

_____

_____

DATE: _____

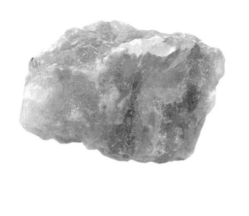

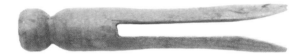

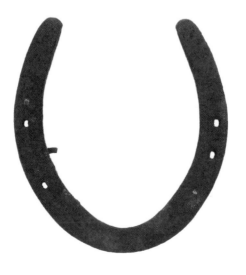

Life will consistently present you with the opportunity to respond differently—to a situation, a person, or even a set of circumstances— until you finally do. The breaking of this pattern is one of life's greatest struggles, but it can be reassuring to know you will be afforded ample opportunities to practice until you get it right.

• • •

one _____

_____

_____

_____

_____

_____

_____

_____

_____

_____

two _____

_____

three

Rituals leave our analytic minds to rest. They allow us to truly feel and discover emotional spaces in ourselves that are only awakened when we perform acts of repetition. Ritual allows us to experience these spaces in solitude or with others; in song or in silence; in prayer or in performance.

• • •

WHAT DID YOU LEARN WHEN YOU MADE TIME FOR RITUAL?

one _____

_____

_____

_____

_____

_____

_____

_____

_____

_____

two _____

_____

_____

three

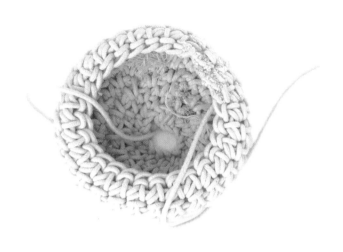

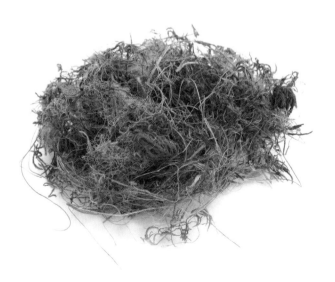

one
_____

_____

_____

_____

_____

two
_____

_____

_____

_____

three
_____

_____

_____

_____

DATE:
_____

There is a distinct difference
between a jump and a fall.
Sometimes the resulting
feelings are similar,
but the intent involved
in the action makes a really
big difference.

WHAT DID YOU LEARN ABOUT YOUR OWN JUMPS AND FALLS?

one

two

three

DATE:

A struggle is just that—a struggle. It doesn't make you stronger or more powerful, and no one will throw you a parade at the end of it.

• • •

one _____

_____

_____

_____

_____

_____

_____

_____

_____

two _____

_____

_____

_____

three

DATE:

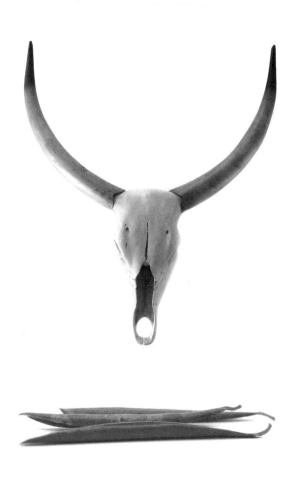
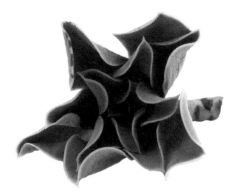

TODAY I LEARNED

one
_____

_____

_____

_____

_____

two
_____

_____

_____

_____

three
_____

_____

_____

_____

DATE: _____

For every two things you are skeptical about, wholeheartedly believe in one thing. Whether it is in love, peace, or unicorns, there is great beauty in letting go and choosing to believe. If this is indeed your one life, spend it not only as a skeptic but also as a believer.

• • •

WHAT DID YOU LEARN WHEN YOU TOOK A LEAP OF FAITH?

one _____

_____

_____

_____

_____

_____

_____

_____

two _____

_____

_____

three

Maintain the right to disappoint people. If we stick ourselves in a box, one rigid with constraints and built on predictability, we don't allow ourselves the possibility of failure. Failure, exhaustive failure, the kind that happens over, and over, and over again, is what leads to creativity and success beyond our wildest dreams.

• • •

WHAT DID YOU LEARN WHEN YOU WERE DISAPPOINTED?

one
_____

_____

_____

_____

_____

_____

_____

_____

_____

two
_____

_____

three

TODAY I LEARNED

one
_____
_____
_____
_____
_____

two
_____
_____
_____
_____

three
_____
_____
_____
_____

DATE: _____

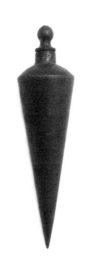

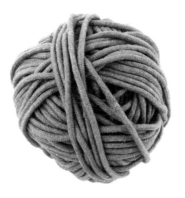

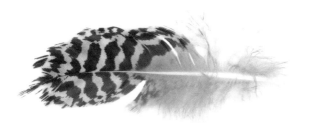

Love, deep and profound love, demands a very
vulnerable and open heart. And it's not just about
the love, but also everything that comes with it—
worry, fear, exhilaration, pride, disappointment,
conflict, humility, and hope. There's no going back,
or stitching the heart closed again; we just get
better at walking around with an open chest.

• • •

**WHAT DID YOU LEARN WHEN YOU OPENED UP
TO THE VULNERABILITY OF LOVE?**

one _____

_____

_____

_____

_____

_____

_____

_____

two _____

_____

_____

three

Speak your tragedy—it lets you know that
you are not alone and it lets your friends,
who aren't ready to speak theirs, know that
they are not alone either.

• • •

**WHAT DID YOU LEARN WHEN YOU OPENED UP
ABOUT SOMETHING PERSONAL?**

one _____

_____

_____

_____

_____

_____

_____

_____

_____

two _____

_____

_____

_____

three

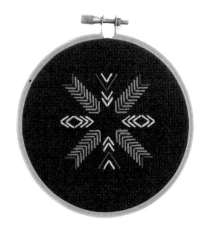

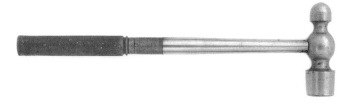

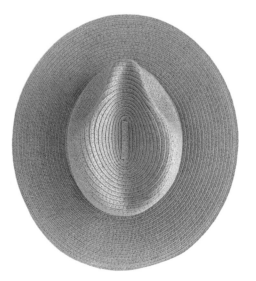

TODAY I LEARNED

one
_____
_____
_____
_____
_____

two
_____
_____
_____
_____

three
_____
_____
_____
_____

DATE:
_____

The beauty of growth is
often equally matched by
the pain of letting go.
Someday before we are
ready, our children will tell us
fewer of their deepest thoughts,
and we will not know as
much as we do now about the
people we love more
than anything. And this
is called growth.

WHAT DID YOU LEARN ABOUT LETTING GO?

one
_____

_____

_____

_____

_____

two
_____

_____

_____

_____

three
_____

_____

_____

_____

DATE: _____

Stay connected no matter what. Whether it is to your body, mind, friends, art, family, music, religion, or practice, pick something and don't let go.
It is this connection that will remain unshakable when the days are long and hard.

• • •

WHAT DID YOU LEARN WHEN YOU CONNECTED WITH SOMETHING OR SOMEONE MEANINGFUL?

one
_____

_____

_____

_____

_____

_____

_____

_____

_____

two
_____

_____

_____

three

DATE:

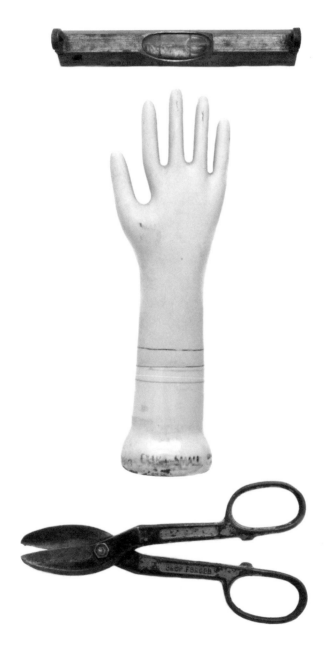

TODAY I LEARNED

one _____

_____

_____

_____

_____

two _____

_____

_____

_____

three _____

_____

_____

_____

DATE: _____

The hard truth is that there is no external pause button. Things don't stop or cease to exist, simply because we have had enough. Things can change, though, and it is in our capacity to be both overwhelmed and persistent. And it's okay to cry through resistance. Action doesn't require a smile.

• • •

WHAT DID YOU LEARN ABOUT OVERCOMING OBSTACLES IN THE MIDST OF CHANGE?

one

_____

_____

_____

_____

_____

_____

_____

_____

_____

two

_____

_____

three

We are beasts of resilience.
We learn to overcome,
to grieve and celebrate all
in one breath, and to
courageously move forward
into uncharted waters.
We are inherently brave.
Remember this.

WHAT DID YOU LEARN ABOUT
YOUR OWN RESILIENCY?

one

_____

_____

_____

_____

_____

two

_____

_____

_____

_____

three

_____

_____

_____

_____

DATE:

_____

Don't rush the foundation. Take your time laying the bricks of your life. This patient work allows for future dreams to come more easily within your grasp.

• • •

WHAT DID YOU LEARN WHEN YOU SLOWED DOWN?

one _____

_____

_____

_____

_____

_____

_____

_____

_____

_____

_____

two _____

_____

_____

_____

three

DATE:

TODAY I LEARNED

one
_____

_____

_____

_____

_____

two
_____

_____

_____

_____

three
_____

_____

_____

_____

DATE:
_____

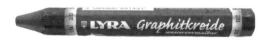

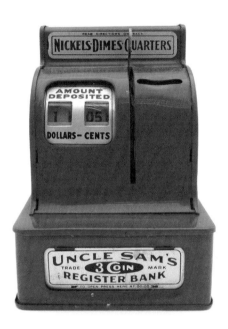

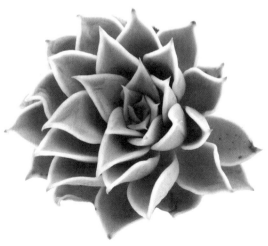

Know the places, people, and sounds you call home. Hold them tightly and refer to these things often, like a compass. They will guide you when you wander astray.

• • •

one _____

_____

_____

_____

_____

_____

_____

_____

_____

two _____

_____

_____

_____

three

Sometimes the right fit can
initially feel all wrong.
Hold fast and trust your path.
Everything needs to
be broken in.

WHAT DID YOU LEARN WHEN YOU WERE OPEN TO GIVING YOUR DECISIONS TIME TO FEEL RIGHT?

one

_____

_____

_____

_____

two

_____

_____

_____

_____

three

_____

_____

_____

_____

DATE: _____

Mark your misery. Have a tangible touchstone to recognize that you survived, and kept on when keepin' on was nearly impossible. Like all things, this time will pass; even when it does, keep something of it with you to help you remember your tenacity.

• • •

WHAT DID YOU LEARN ABOUT YOUR STRENGTH?

one
_____

_____

_____

_____

_____

_____

_____

_____

two
_____

_____

_____

three

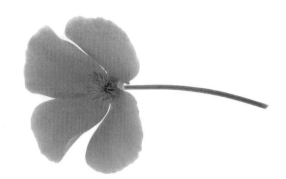

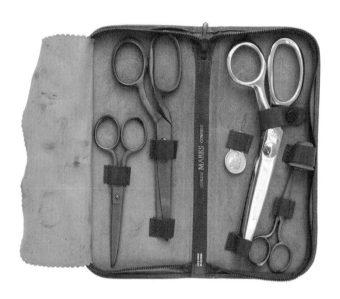

TODAY I LEARNED

one
_____
_____
_____
_____
_____

two
_____
_____
_____
_____

three
_____
_____
_____
_____

DATE: _____

Sometimes the loveliest moments are best kept private. In a world of documenting and sharing absolutely anything and everything, know when a moment is so precious it deserves to be just that—a moment.

• • •

WHAT DID YOU LEARN WHEN YOU STAYED IN THE PRESENT MOMENT?

one

_____

_____

_____

_____

_____

_____

_____

_____

_____

two

_____

_____

_____

_____

three

Be Kind. That's it really.
Kindness is not
complicated, or deep,
nor does it need
a prerequisite.
Kindness is a just and
equal offering.
We all have the ability
to be kind, so do it
and do it often.

WHAT DID YOU LEARN WHEN YOU STARTED
FROM A PLACE OF KINDNESS?

one
_____

_____

_____

_____

_____

two
_____

_____

_____

_____

three
_____

_____

_____

_____

DATE:
_____

If you are going to be afraid of anything, you might as well be afraid of everything. Fear thrives on contagion. It counts on us to compare and contrast. Being afraid of one thing often leads to being fearful of three or four more.

• • •

**WHAT DID YOU LEARN WHEN YOU CHOSE
TO FACE FEAR HEAD-ON?**

one
_____

_____

_____

_____

_____

_____

_____

_____

two
_____

_____

_____

_____

three

TODAY I LEARNED

one
_____

_____

_____

_____

_____

two
_____

_____

_____

_____

three
_____

_____

_____

_____

DATE:
_____

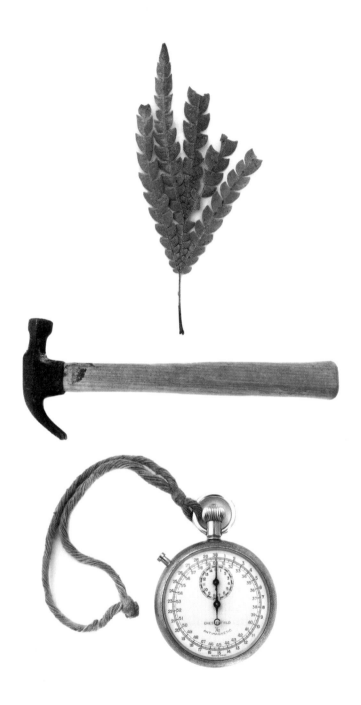

A win is still a win. Even when your win is not by a landslide, but by the skin of your teeth; when it is in inches instead of yards, in extra innings, in overtime, or by default. Even if it all goes down differently than you had imagined, and you wonder why you are still in this fight, a win is still a win.

• • •

WHAT DID YOU LEARN ABOUT YOUR OWN FIGHT FOR SUCCESS?

one
_____

_____

_____

_____

_____

_____

_____

_____

_____

two
_____

_____

_____

three

Discover what holds
you when no one and
nothing else can.
Know your grounding
force and keep it close.
Invite it over often and
never let go.

WHAT DID YOU LEARN ABOUT
WHAT COMFORTS YOU?

one
_____

_____

_____

_____

_____

two
_____

_____

_____

_____

_____

three
_____

_____

_____

_____

_____

DATE:
_____

TODAY I LEARNED

one
_____

_____

_____

_____

_____

two
_____

_____

_____

_____

three
_____

_____

_____

_____

DATE: _____

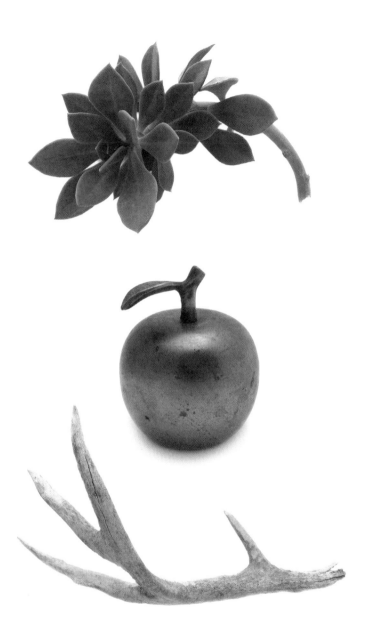

Make it fun. We can't control what comes at us, so let's get really good at making what we can control fun. Celebrate Wednesday with a cake.

• • •

WHAT DID YOU LEARN WHEN YOU MADE THE ORDINARY FUN?

one _____

_____

_____

_____

_____

_____

_____

_____

_____

two _____

_____

_____

_____

three

There is no amount of love that can convince
someone to do something they are not ready for.
Perhaps this is one of the greatest challenges of
love. We just have to wait.

• • •

one

_____

_____

_____

_____

_____

_____

_____

_____

_____

two

_____

_____

_____

three

DATE:

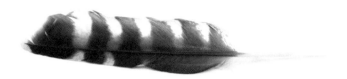

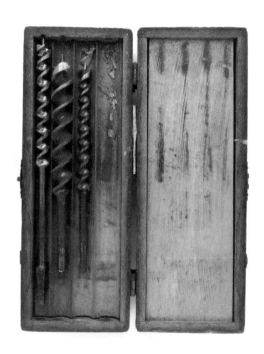

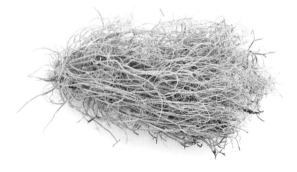

TODAY I LEARNED

one _____

_____

_____

_____

_____

two _____

_____

_____

_____

_____

three _____

_____

_____

_____

_____

DATE: _____

There will be times when you will feel lonely in a crowd, poor surrounded by riches, compromised when strong, and like a total and complete failure in the midst of great success. When your feelings don't match the facts, look within, and remember you've walked through fire before.

• • •

WHAT DID YOU LEARN WHEN YOU SEPARATED FACT FROM FEELING?

one _____

_____

_____

_____

_____

_____

_____

_____

two _____

_____

_____

three

Sometimes there is
only darkness in darkness.
Luckily, our eyes adjust.

WHAT DID YOU LEARN ABOUT FINDING
YOUR WAY THROUGH THE DARK?

one _____

_____

_____

_____

_____

two _____

_____

_____

_____

three _____

_____

_____

_____

DATE: _____

Break free from the attitude of "all or nothing."
There is much to be gained from things achieved
at 50% capacity. Some is better than none
and can often lead us back to all.

• • •

**WHAT DID YOU LEARN WHEN YOU HONORED
YOUR CURRENT CAPACITY?**

one
_____

_____

_____

_____

_____

_____

_____

_____

_____

two
_____

_____

_____

_____

three

TODAY I LEARNED

one
_____

_____

_____

_____

_____

two
_____

_____

_____

_____

three
_____

_____

_____

_____

_____

DATE: _____

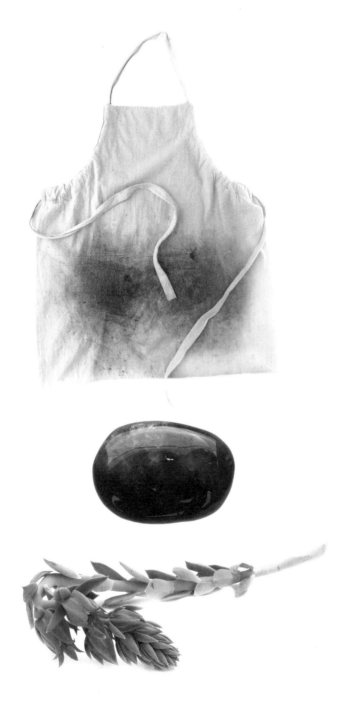

When it comes to your purpose, learn how to respond to the word "no." You will face a seemingly unending labyrinth of "nos" along the way to your ultimate destination. Learn how to crawl under, climb over, and run right through them. Believe in the beauty and essential worthiness of your purpose.

• • •

WHAT DID YOU LEARN WHEN YOU CHALLENGED REJECTION?

one _____

_____

_____

_____

_____

_____

_____

_____

_____

two _____

_____

three

Run toward what scares you. Learn to examine, go deep, be in the darkness, taste it, love it, and be less afraid, knowing that any struggle you face is really leading you toward something worthwhile.

• • •

WHAT DID YOU LEARN WHEN YOU MOVED TOWARD INSTEAD OF AWAY FROM SOMETHING?

one _____

_____

_____

_____

_____

_____

_____

_____

_____

two _____

_____

_____

_____

three

TODAY I LEARNED

one
_____

_____

_____

_____

_____

two
_____

_____

_____

_____

three
_____

_____

_____

_____

_____

DATE:
_____

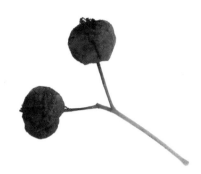

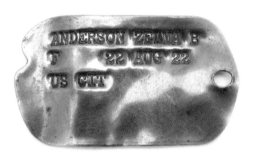

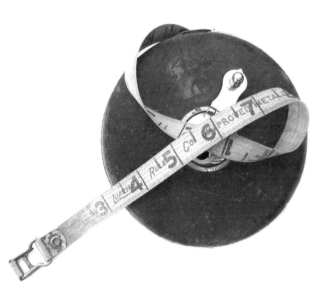

There is just one road.
It is yours, and there are
no wrong turns because
you have carved its
path before you all along.

WHAT DID YOU LEARN ABOUT
MAKING CHOICES?

one
_____

_____

_____

_____

_____

two
_____

_____

_____

_____

three
_____

_____

_____

_____

_____

DATE:
_____

If you choose to keep enemies, choose them wisely, for they will define you.

• • •

WHAT DID YOU LEARN ABOUT YOURSELF FROM YOUR GREATEST OPPONENTS?

one
_____

_____

_____

_____

_____

_____

_____

_____

_____

_____

two
_____

_____

_____

_____

three

Acknowledge the importance of what we leave behind. The little things we call incidentals— a loved one's pair of glasses, a hairbrush— suddenly have meaning in someone's absence. Embrace the way these things matter.

• • •

one
_____

_____

_____

_____

_____

_____

_____

_____

_____

two
_____

_____

_____

three

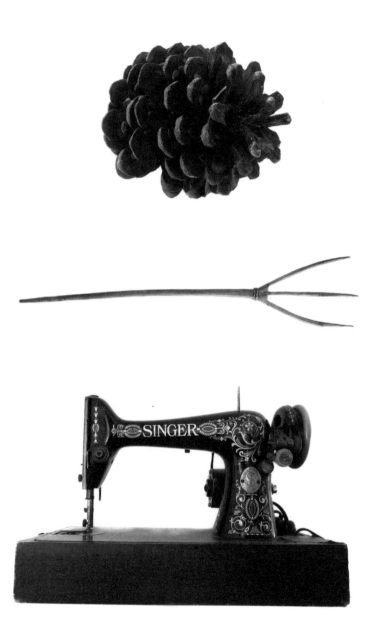

TODAY I LEARNED

one
_____

_____

_____

_____

_____

two
_____

_____

_____

_____

three
_____

_____

_____

_____

DATE:
_____

Learn to master the ordinary. The extreme highs
and lows of life may require more of our attention,
but the rest—that's the gold. The ordinary is
where we spend most of our time. Discover
happiness in these everyday moments.

• • •

**WHAT DID YOU LEARN FROM THE
ORDINARY MOMENTS?**

one
_____

_____

_____

_____

_____

_____

_____

_____

_____

two
_____

_____

_____

three

DATE:

Some changes are welcome and made willingly. Other changes are fought with every single cell of our bodies. Nevertheless, jump when you are able, fall when necessary, and learn to bend with incredible flexibility. Relish the softness that is and always will be the gift of the human condition.

• • •

WHAT DID YOU LEARN ABOUT YOUR OWN SOFTNESS?

one _____

_____

_____

_____

_____

_____

_____

_____

_____

_____

two _____

_____

_____

three

TODAY I LEARNED

one
_____
_____
_____
_____
_____

two
_____
_____
_____
_____

three
_____
_____
_____
_____
_____

DATE:
_____

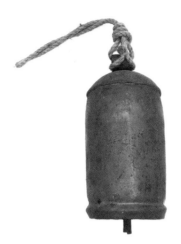

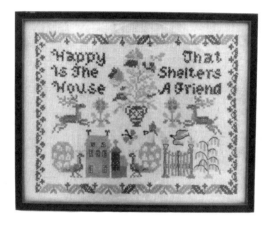

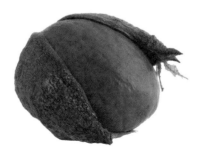

Your sensitivity is a gift.
It is your breath, your blood,
your rare ability to be not
only in a moment but in
harmony with a moment.
What feels vulnerable now
is your greatest asset showing
itself so strongly that it
refuses to remain a secret.

WHAT DID YOU LEARN WHEN YOU ALLOWED
YOUR SENSITIVITY TO EMERGE?

one
_____

_____

_____

_____

_____

two
_____

_____

_____

_____

three
_____

_____

_____

_____

DATE:
_____

Do the work. Lists are nice and goals can be grand, but they don't mean a thing without action. Change—deep, meaningful, transformative change—rarely happens in a series of minutes, or hours, or days. It takes numerous starts and stops, successes and failures, and sometimes just pure and inexplicable faith. Relax, because evolution takes a lifetime.

• • •

WHAT DID YOU LEARN WHEN YOU PUT SOMETHING IMPORTANT INTO ACTION?

one _____

_____

_____

_____

_____

_____

_____

_____

two _____

_____

three

TODAY I LEARNED

one _____

_____

_____

_____

_____

two _____

_____

_____

_____

three _____

_____

_____

_____

_____

DATE: _____

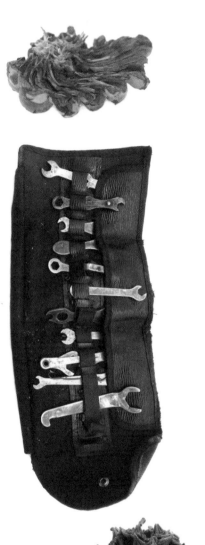
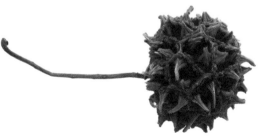

Learn to take a metaphorical punch.
Most things worth fighting for in life are well
worth the bruise. Embrace that it's not all
going to be easy or happen on the first try.
"Eventually" is very different from "never."

• • •

**WHAT DID YOU LEARN WHEN YOU
WERE PATIENT?**

one _____

_____

_____

_____

_____

_____

_____

_____

_____

two _____

_____

_____

three

Let people in.
Give them a chance
to surprise you.

WHAT DID YOU LEARN WHEN YOU
GAVE SOMEONE A CHANCE?

one
_____

_____

_____

_____

_____

two
_____

_____

_____

_____

three
_____

_____

_____

_____

DATE:
_____

Keep your sense of humor no matter what.
There is incredible grace in laughing through
the tough times. When the world pushes
down upon you with immense weight,
remember the strength of laughter.

• • •

**WHAT DID YOU LEARN WHEN YOU
FOUND HUMOR IN SOMETHING?**

one _____

_____

_____

_____

_____

_____

_____

_____

_____

two _____

_____

_____

three

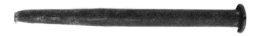

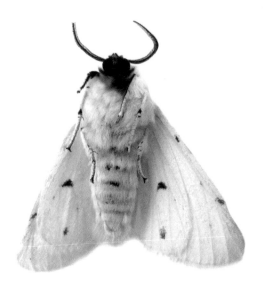

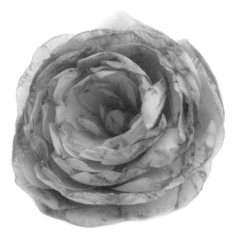

TODAY I LEARNED

one
_____

_____

_____

_____

_____

two
_____

_____

_____

_____

three
_____

_____

_____

_____

_____

DATE:
_____

It is possible to gain from the lessons you never asked for, even if all you learn is that you hated every minute of it. Often knowing what you don't want sets you in the clear direction of what you wish for.

• • •

WHAT DID YOU LEARN FROM WHAT YOU DON'T WANT?

one _____

_____

_____

_____

_____

_____

_____

_____

_____

two _____

_____

_____

three

The future is a story.
There is no outcome set
in stone, and no plan that
has been fully realized.
The tides can always turn,
even with the smallest
of paddles.

WHAT DID YOU LEARN ABOUT THE STORIES
YOU TELL ABOUT THE FUTURE?

one
_____

_____

_____

_____

_____

two
_____

_____

_____

_____

three
_____

_____

_____

_____

_____

DATE:
_____

TODAY I LEARNED

one _____

_____

_____

_____

_____

two _____

_____

_____

_____

_____

three _____

_____

_____

_____

_____

DATE: _____

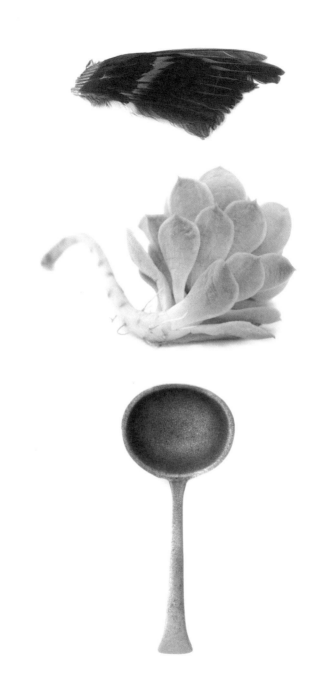

Most moments are roller coasters,
full of highs and lows. That split second at
the very top of the ride, right before the plunge,
is when you can see everything laid out before
you. In that moment there is the chance
to scream, or laugh, or both. Do both.

• • •

**WHAT DID YOU LEARN WHEN YOU ALLOWED
YOURSELF TO ENJOY THE RIDE?**

one
_____

_____

_____

_____

_____

_____

_____

_____

_____

two
_____

_____

three

It's all about experience.
Experience provides a magic
that requires patience.
Learn to love that.

HOW DID YOUR EXPERIENCE GUIDE YOU
IN SURPRISING WAYS?

one

_____

_____

_____

_____

_____

two

_____

_____

_____

_____

_____

three

_____

_____

_____

_____

DATE: _____

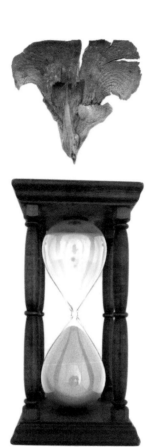

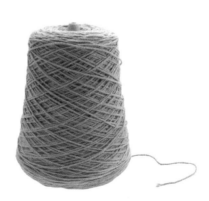